ANDREW MARVELL

Selected Poems

Edited with an introduction by Bill Hutchings

FyfieldBooks

ISBN: 0-85635-258-6

First published in 1979
Published in new format in 1988 by
Carcanet Press Limited
208–212 Corn Exchange Buildings
Manchester M4 3BQ

The publisher acknowledges financial assistance
from the Arts Council of Great Britain.

Printed in England by SRP Ltd, Exeter.

CONTENTS

INTRODUCTION

EVER since his *Miscellaneous Poems* were published in 1681, three years after his death, the progress of Andrew Marvell's fortunes has been curious. That volume was prefaced with the words of one Mary Marvell, informing the reader that the poems 'are printed according to the exact copies of my late dear husband'; but Marvell seems never to have married. The title-page of the 1681 Folio described the author as a late member of the honourable House of Commons; and indeed, it was for his political activities that Marvell was best known for a century after his death. Although editions of his works, including the lyric poems, came out in 1726 and 1776, he was primarily noted as a champion of liberty and an author of satirical works until the early nineteenth century, when admiring references to the poetry were made by William Lisle Bowles, William Hazlitt, Charles Lamb and James Leigh Hunt.

In the twentieth century, Marvell's reputation has soared. An influential essay by T. S. Eliot appeared in 1921; the 'metaphysical poets' (among whom, for better or worse, Marvell has so often been placed) grew in critical popularity; and subsequently a flurry of academic treatises has ensured a lengthy bibliography in any new work on Marvell. The benefits of this growth in interest are obvious: an increase in knowledge is never to be spurned. But some of the results seem designed to persuade us that the latest stage in Marvell's fortunes is the most curious. The eighteenth-century neglect was far from universal; and the nineteenth-century observers, vague though they often are, seem to have used appropriate words ('sweetness', 'witty delicacy', 'pleasant', 'lively'). When one reads some modern criticism (a recent example informs us that Marvell's poetry is 'allegorical in that its explicit subject matter is not its main concern'*), one's heart tends to leap down. This is rather odd when the poetry itself seems so obviously designed to make one's heart leap up.

One of the most curious, and damaging, effects of some modern approaches to Marvell is that a small output of poems, most of them short, has been so often left struggling to escape from a weight of

---

*Bruce King, *Marvell's Allegorical Poetry* (1977), p. 10.

immensely knowledgeable exegesis. A heavy hand is exactly the opposite of what one needs when reading something like this:

> To make a final conquest of all me,
> Love did compose so sweet an enemy,
> In whom both beauties to my death agree,
> Joining themselves in fatal harmony;
> That while she with her eyes my heart does bind,
> She with her voice might captivate my mind.

('The Fair Singer', 1—6)

This seems immediately attractive poetry. In tone, one might call it playful: taking a common enough idea, Marvell gives it an added humour by seeing the poet as subjected to a double assault. In keeping with this exaggeration, the language comically extends the stock 'conquest' of love into the succession of 'enemy', 'death', 'fatal', 'bind', 'captivate'. The cunning use of 'captivate' ('fascinate' and 'take captive') goes with the musical play on 'compose' and 'harmony'.

A useful comparison is with a poem by Edmund Waller, a contemporary of Marvell. Here we find the same notion, that a singer's beauty and voice combine forces to enchant the poet:

> Behold, and listen, while the fair
> Breaks in sweet sounds the willing air,
> And with her own breath fans the fire
> Which her bright eyes do first inspire.
> What reason can that love control,
> Which more than one way courts the soul?

('Of Mrs Arden', 1—6)

There are, certainly, differences between Marvell's lines and Waller's. Waller is more obviously 'lyrical' (the lines are shorter and have more metrical regularity) and rhetorical: where he demands and questions, Marvell seems to state and meditate. But there are also similarities: both poets clearly delight in exploring a nice, whimsical idea, and both express it with directness and clarity. Wit, that is, is controlled by calm and careful verbal felicity.

Yet Waller's fortunes have followed a very different course from Marvell's. Very fashionable in the seventeenth century (the playwrights Etherege and Congreve make characters quote him), he was still highly regarded in the eighteenth century, but has since descended into relative (and, one might add, unjust) neglect. Why, then, does the twentieth century rate the two poets as it does? The answer, I suspect, is that one finds in Marvell a certain awareness of social or moral issues, a certain 'seriousness', which has its appeal to a modern audience. But we should not ignore that Marvell has in common with Waller (and other seventeenth-century poets, such as Lovelace, Carew and Suckling) qualities of witty elegance, of graceful humour, the characteristics of a style one might call 'cavalier'. It is the combination of these two apparently conflicting elements which, I should like to suggest, gives to Marvell's poetry its particular effect.

Andrew Marvell was born on 31 March 1621 at Winestead-in-Holderness, near Hull. His father had held the living of Winestead since 1614, and, in 1624, was appointed lecturer in Holy Trinity Church, Hull. Marvell attended Hull Grammar School until 1633 when he went to Trinity College, Cambridge. He stayed there for seven years, save for a brief flirtation with Catholicism and London, where, according to family tradition, his father found him and returned him to Cambridge. During the years of the civil war, Marvell went on a grand tour of Holland, France, Italy and Spain. He had already written some poems when, in 1651, he went to live as tutor to Mary, the daughter of General Fairfax, who had resigned after being commander-in-chief of the parliamentary forces. Marvell stayed at Fairfax's Nunappleton estate for about two years, and it is probable that most of his non-satirical poetry was written during this time. Fairfax, a man of culture as well as a soldier, certainly exerted an influence on Marvell: two of his poems are directly addressed to the general.

The rest of Marvell's life is mainly a matter of political involvement. In 1653 John Milton, then Secretary for Foreign Languages, recommended him for his own assistant. Although this appointment was not made, Marvell was appointed Latin Secretary in 1657, after a spell as tutor to William Dutton, who became a ward of Cromwell. Marvell had by now been using his pen in support of Cromwell. He was elected Member of Parliament for Hull after Cromwell's death, a position he held until his own death. After the restoration of the monarchy, he travelled in Europe and wrote at home, this time verse satires and prose tracts, of which the most substantial is *The Rehearsal Transpros'd* (part one 1672; part two 1673). This was written against Samuel Parker, an Anglican polemicist who had attacked freedom of religious conscience and had supported absolute government. Marvell died in 1678.

Marvell's age was one of unrest and upheaval. In 'Upon Appleton House', the poet goes on a tour of Fairfax's estate. He comes upon a scene of hay-making:

The mower now commands the field;
In whose new traverse seemeth wrought
A camp of battle newly fought:
Where, as the meads with hay, the plain
Lies quilted o'er with bodies slain:
The women that with forks it fling,
Do represent the pillaging.   (418-424)

Marvell's method is one of imaginative upheaval: the poet's eye translates pastoral activities into military activities, with obvious contemporary reverberations. A walk through a country estate leads into what is, one would think, virtually an opposite vision. This process operates throughout the poem: awareness of one thing is countered by the intrusion of that which seems very different, and yet turns out to be very close. Here are the flowers in Fairfax's garden imitating their owner's former military life, firing their odours as if weapons: 'These, as their Governor goes by,/ In fragrant volleys they let fly' (297-8). Fairfax has renounced one form of life, and has sought retirement. Yet the poet cannot refrain from describing Fairfax's present in the language of his past. Is the result of this clash a feeling that the general's new life is absurdly beneath his former status, or that his new environment creates pleasure while his martial past destroyed life? Is the humour working to his advantage or his disadvantage?

Marvell seems to play with the issue, and then to step back, leaving his reader teased by the problem. This habit operates throughout his poetry. Here is a stanza from 'The Garden':

> What wondrous life in this I lead!
> Ripe apples drop about my head;
> The luscious clusters of the vine
> Upon my mouth do crush their wine;
> The nectarine, and curious peach,
> Into my hands themselves do reach;
> Stumbling on melons, as I pass,
> Ensnared with flowers, I fall on grass. (33-40)

As William Empson pointed out in his essay on 'The Garden' in *Some Versions of Pastoral*, the stanza begins with apples and ends with a fall; moreover, 'melon' is the Greek word for 'apple', so there are two lots of apples assailing the poet. Does the stanza, then, record an experience related to the original fall of man, with the poet as Adam? But the experience is, indeed, 'wondrous': nature seems to involve the poet in its embraces. So, if this is a physical experience, man's role is oddly passive. Whether it's the fall of man, or a vision of animated nature, there's still the question of whether we take the stanza 'seriously' or regard the poet's plight as ludicrous.

The point, I think, is that all these possibilities are there: the clipped couplets, precise and cool, play off against the wide-ranging implications of the words. Similarly, the 'fragrant volleys' which fire at Fairfax make him both attractive and rather absurd. One of the issues in 'Upon Appleton House' is whether Fairfax was right or wrong to retire from public life; and, hence, whether retirement is a justifiable course of action. The subject was by no means novel when Marvell chose it: indeed, he is throughout his poetry more a modifier of existing traditions than an innovator. But many other writers, both before and after Marvell, saw the issue in pretty straightforward terms: the world of war or business was morally corrupt (or just plain unpleasant), so that retirement to a life of tranquil contemplation in the countryside was clearly to be preferred for the good of one's soul (or just for one's safety). Marvell refuses to present such a simple, one-sided view. Thus he can testify to the moral excellence of Fairfax's decision, telling us that he preferred conscience to ambition (stanza 45), and he can also give us a picture of the once-great general surveying the 'half-dry trenches' of his garden while England descends into chaos (stanza 44). Marvell

11

can get away with this because Fairfax's qualities are shown as so great that he is ideally suited to both roles, that of the moral solitary and that of the active repairer of the country's ills.

This shifting attitude to the subject-matter of the poem is reflected in what Marvell asks his reader's attitude to be. Sometimes our response may simply alternate along with the poet's; but more often the effect is more complex because the tone of the verse defies our attempts to pin it down. This is where T. S. Eliot's definition of the wit as 'a tough reasonableness beneath the slight lyric grace' has the unfortunate effect of suggesting that there are definable strata, as if we dig through the lyric grace to the really substantial layer beneath. The fifth stanza of 'The Garden', which I quoted earlier, seems to me to contrive to be playful and 'tough' at the same time, as it combines ecstasy with absurdity, morality with sensual indulgence.

Here's another short example from Marvell's other poem to Fairfax, 'Upon the Hill and Grove at Bilbrough'. Once the general won his laurels in military victories; now the only trees to reward him are those which grow on Bilbrough Hill, one of his favourite places of retirement. Marvell imagines those trees expressing their own feeling of inadequacy: 'Through groves of pikes he thundered then,/ And mountains raised of dying men' (67-8). The trees say this in a tone of admiration, but the phrase which completes the couplet refuses to be tied down by that one tone. Yet the poet goes on to confirm the inadequacy of the trees which are Fairfax's chosen environment. Typical here is the way in which the same language expresses contraries: 'grove' is both the trees and soldiers' raised pikes; and 'mountain' is both the hill and a heap of bodies. Words themselves slide around: just as the poet in 'Upon Appleton House' cannot see haymaking without imagining a battle-field, so here single words cannot resist their possible other meaning. Marvell, detached and sophisticated, teases his reader with the dual nature of images, of language, of his subject.

As an attempt at a definition of this effect of Marvell's poetry, the most useful I have found is that suggested by Arnold Hauser in *Mannerism: The Crisis of the Renaissance and the Origin of Modern Art*, and taken up by Louis L. Martz in *The Wit of Love*. Mannerism is a term used in art history, and, like all such terms, needs to be treated with especial care when it is applied to literature. Nevertheless, Hauser's explanation of what he sees as the mannerist qualities contains much that seems to illuminate Marvell's poetry. He mentions, for example, playfulness and a love of paradoxes and contrasts. Particularly suggestive is his definition of the principle he sees as underlying the mannerist outlook, 'the permanent ambiguity of all things, great and small, and . . . the impossibility of attaining certainty about anything' (I, 13). In this view, the opposite of every truth is itself true: every coin has its other, and equally valid, face. If to this is added another feature of mannerist art, its attention to style (the word, incidentally, comes from the Italian word, 'maniera', meaning 'style'), a concern with gracefulness of surface texture, then the result seems curiously appropriate to the combination of what I call the cavalier qualities of Marvell's verse and its particular, even idiosyncratic, treatment of its subjects.

Let's move on to a poem I haven't yet mentioned, 'An Horatian Ode upon Cromwell's Return from Ireland'. The title of the poem is doubly significant. The choice of Cromwell inverts the situation in the Fairfax poems: the subject is not a retired man, but a man committed to action. But, also, the form of the ode is Horatian (the stanza form itself imitates one of Horace's stanza forms, with two longer followed by two shorter lines); that is, cool and sophisticated in tone, not irrepressibly enthusiastic like the Pindaric ode. This initial paradox, a cool poem about a violent subject, leads straight into the opening lines:

> The forward youth that would appear
> Must now forsake his muses dear,
>> Nor in the shadows sing
>> His numbers languishing.
> 'Tis time to leave the books in dust,
> And oil the unused armour's rust:
>> Removing from the wall
>> The corslet of the hall.   (1-8)

The critic Cleanth Brooks suggested that 'forward' was the first of a series of ambiguities in the poem, and he thereby set off a battle of interpretations. If 'forward' has a possible implication of 'presumptuous' as well as simply 'high-spirited', then an undercurrent of criticism of Cromwell and the life of action may be under way, even as the poem appears to be advocating such a life. Yet there is a more immediately potent paradox in the lines. It is curious that this call to arms and dismissal of poetry comes right at the beginning of a poem (and one which is a hundred and twenty lines long). So the writer says that it's time to stop writing just as he starts to write. Furthermore, we, the readers, are involved in the contradiction: we are told that it's time to 'leave the books in dust' just as we've started to read. But, because the poem does not end here, we go on reading. Marvell is not simply playing a game with us (though I think he is doing that), but he is revealing something paradoxical in the nature of language: how does one use words to say that now is not the time for words? But, conversely, how else can one say it? This opening is really a controlled explosion, establishing a starting-point for a poem in praise of Cromwell which has, at its very centre, an apparently sympathetic account of Charles I's dignity when confronting the scaffold.

One should beware of equating these qualities of Marvell's poetry with indifference: the detached, controlled style holds together an involvement in the complexities of language and of what language can be used to talk about. A reading of 'To his Coy Mistress' will dispel any feeling that Marvell is only ever luke-warm: 'Had we but world enough, and time,/ This coyness lady were no crime' (1-2). Given an almost unlimited span of time and space, love could be taken gently and easily. It's clear enough that, once again, Marvell is working within a well-worn tradition: he is setting up the 'carpe diem' ('seize the day') notion, and it really comes as no surprise when the poem changes key: 'But at my back I always hear/ Time's winged chariot hurrying near' (21-2). Life, we know, is not kind enough to allow us all the time and space we want: pleasure, therefore, has to be seized, even to be pursued. Much of the poem's intensity derives from its cruelty. Death does not remain an abstract concept, but is confronted in the physical horror of worms trying the dead mistress's virginity. Nor is there any refusal to tackle the harsh reality involved even in seizing the day: pleasures must be torn 'with rough strife,/ Thorough the iron gates of life' (an image just as physical and brutal as that of the worms).

Yet the longest of the poem's three sections is the first. Marvell is not merely establishing the unreality as an Aunt Sally to be knocked down by 'But at my back . . . ':

Thou by the Indian Ganges' side
Shouldst rubies find: I by the tide
Of Humber would complain . . .   (5-7)

This is a joke directed at the poet himself (Marvell's home town, we recall, was Hull); but it is also a marvellous compliment to the mistress. She is, the poet implies, worthy of such exotic surroundings; and she is the sort who would just light upon precious stones. Such idealism is her due: 'you deserve this state'. So the poet is telling the mistress not to behave in the way she really ought to behave: her coyness is both appropriate and inappropriate. This paradox creates much of the tension which sustains the poem.

'To his Coy Mistress' is not alone in deriving its strength from a tension between different parts of the poem. It is significant that some of Marvell's poems are in the form of dialogue, with points of view playing off against each other. 'A Dialogue Between the Resolved Soul, and Created Pleasure' and 'A Dialogue between the Soul and Body' are perhaps the most striking examples, but a similar pattern is found in 'Clorinda and Damon', 'A Dialogue between Thyrsis and Dorinda', and 'Ametas and Thestylis making Hay-Ropes'. In these three poems Marvell uses another traditional *genre*, that of the pastoral; but, as ever, he gives it his own particular development.

In 'Clorinda and Damon', for example, Clorinda tries to persuade the shepherd, Damon, to join her in some pastoral love-making. Despite Clorinda's adoption of the 'carpe diem' theme ('Seize the short joys then, ere they vade'), Damon resolutely refuses, talking instead of heaven and virtue. When Clorinda demands an explanation, she is told that meeting the god, Pan, has changed Damon's life: he can no longer sing of the things shepherds are supposed to sing of, but only of Pan. Concord follows from this:

C. Sweet must Pan sound in Damon's note.
D. Clorinda's voice might make it sweet.
C. Who would not in Pan's praises meet?   (24-6)

Pan is the presiding deity of shepherds, and thus fits the pastoral setting as well as carrying the Christian use of 'shepherd'. Also, the god's name derives from the Greek word for 'all', so it appropriately encompasses diversity within a unity. Yet Clorinda seems more concerned about how sweet Damon's music will be, and he is quick to bring her into harmony with a compliment. The suggestions of personal attitudes are sustained even within the apparently religious resolution. Through Marvell's wit, musical harmony becomes a means of keeping such a tension in a low key: in praising Pan, Clorinda and Damon 'meet' as they had not before, and the result is music ('all the world is our Pan's choir').

Even when there is no dialogue, parts of the poems often play off against each other structurally, as in 'To his Coy Mistress'. The most splendid example of this is 'The Gallery', a poem oddly neglected by most critics, although it seems to me quintessentially Marvellian. The idea is that the poet turns his soul into a picture gallery in which are hung paintings of his Clora in her varying poses and attitudes. Stanzas two, three, four and five describe the pictures in a tautly conceived representation of the poet's conflicting reactions to her.

First she is humorously exaggerated as 'an inhuman murderess', cruelly testing the hearts of men with her instruments of torture, 'Black eyes, red lips, and curled hair'. Stanza three shows the very opposite of this: instead of being actively destructive, she is passively inviting: 'When in the east she slumbering lies,/ And stretches out her milky thighs' (19-20). She is now not dressed as a tyrant, but as a goddess, 'Aurora in the dawn'. Love in stanza two is destructive and cynical; in stanza three it is 'harmless' and idealistic. As we move on to the next picture, we find ourselves confronted with the result of the first picture: Clora is now an enchantress, actively vexing the ghost of her murdered lover. Correspondingly, the fourth picture reverts to the mythological idealism of the second, turning Clora into the goddess of love. She is passive once again ('thou sit'st afloat'), and enchanting in a more pleasant sense than in the preceding picture. This series of paintings represents Clora's ability 'Either to please me, or torment': the contradictions are all true, for every picture has its equally valid opposite. But the poem has to end satisfactorily somehow. Marvell chooses as his device for so doing not a chorus (as in the 'Resolved Soul and Created Pleasure' and

'Clorinda and Damon'), nor a low-key retreat (as in 'Upon Appleton House'), but a surprise:

> But, of these pictures and the rest,
> That at the entrance likes me best:
> Where the same posture, and the look
> Remains, with which I first was took.
> A tender shepherdess, whose hair
> Hangs loosely playing in the air,
> Transplanting flowers from the green hill,
> To crown her head, and bosom fill. (49-56)

This picture has no direct opposite. It is an assertion of pastoral ideals whereby woman and nature may exist in perfect harmony: her hair (loose and natural, not curled as in stanza two) plays in the air, and flowers are transplanted to decorate her head and bosom. This marvellously rounds off the poem, but leaves the contradictions where they were. For this last picture is really the first: the ideal can only exist in the present as retrospection.

I called this conclusion a device: it's a brilliant contrivance to resolve the poem without really resolving it. At the beginning the poet asks Clora to look at the gallery of his soul and say whether he has 'contrived it well'. At the end, we, as the viewers of the poem, see how Marvell has 'contrived it well'. Contrivance, a self-conscious demonstration of sheer artistry, is a cavalier quality, at one with elegance and grace. Finally, I think, one has always to return to the surface qualities of Marvell's poetry which hold the tensions within an artistic whole. 'The Coronet' depends on a paradox which demonstrates this point. Here the poet expresses his desire to renounce elaborate pastoral love poetry ('the fragrant towers/ That once adorned my shepherdess's head') and instead write in honour of his Saviour. But the materials for that creation are of this world, for man belongs to this world. All the poet can do is gather flowers, objects caught in our cycle of growth and decay, whether they be to adorn a shepherdess or Christ. Realizing this, the poet asks Christ to rid his poems of the presence of evil:

> But Thou who only couldst the serpent tame,
> Either his slippery knots at once untie,
> And disentangle all his winding snare:

Or shatter too with him my curious frame:
And let these wither, so that he may die,
Though set with skill and chosen out with care.
That they, while Thou on both their spoils dost tread,
May crown thy feet, that could not crown thy head.

(19-26)

In order to express this plea, Marvell has himself built another 'curious' (i.e. elaborately, carefully made) frame, the poem called 'The Coronet'. All is carefully ordered, up to the last refusal to relinquish completely the idea of a crown (which was where the poem began). Thus the inadequacy of man's creations is asserted in a poem which is itself 'set with skill and chosen out with care', a poem which thereby declares man's continuing aspiration to perfection. The paradoxes, the contradictions go on, but so does their exquisite frame.

A NOTE ON THE TEXT

The texts of the poems in this selection are based on the 1681 Folio (*Miscellaneous Poems*). Spelling has been modernized, except where to do so would destroy the text utterly. The original punctuation is retained, as is the order of the poems.

There are a number of textual problems in Marvell. Whenever emendation proved necessary, I have chosen what seems to me the least complicated option. For example, lines 33-4 of 'To his Coy Mistress' read in the Folio: 'Now therefore, while the youthful hew/ Sits on thy skin like morning glew'. Various suggestions have been made for emendation, such as reading 'lew' (meaning 'warmth') instead of 'glew', retaining 'glew' (citing more obscure senses of the word than the obvious one), and using a manuscript reading which has 'youthful glew' and 'morning dew'. Thomas Cooke, an eighteenth-century editor, retained the Folio version, with the substitution of 'dew' for 'glew'. This seems to me the neatest and most satisfactory solution. Readers wishing to follow up such problems are referred to the standard edition: *The Poems and Letters of Andrew Marvell*, ed. H. M. Margoliouth, 2 vols. (1927); 3rd edition, revised Pierre Legouis with the collaboration of E. E. Duncan Jones, 2 vols. (1971).

A DIALOGUE BETWEEN THE RESOLVED SOUL, AND CREATED PLEASURE

Courage my soul, now learn to wield
The weight of thine immortal shield.
Close on thy head thy helmet bright.
Balance thy sword against the fight.
See where an army, strong as fair,
With silken banners spreads the air.
Now, if thou be'st that thing divine,
In this day's combat let it shine:
And show that nature wants an art
10   To conquer one resolved heart.

Pleasure
Welcome the creation's guest,
Lord of earth, and heaven's heir.
Lay aside that warlike crest,
And of nature's banquet share:
Where the souls of fruits and flowers
Stand prepared to heighten yours.

Soul
I sup above, and cannot stay
To bait so long upon the way.

Pleasure
On these downy pillows lie,
20   Whose soft plumes will thither fly:
On these roses strewed so plain
Lest one leaf thy side should strain.

Soul
My gentler rest is on a thought,
Conscious of doing what I ought.

Pleasure
If thou be'st with perfumes pleased,
Such as oft the gods appeased,
Thou in fragrant clouds shalt show
Like another god below.

Soul
A soul that knows not to presume
30   Is heaven's and its own perfume.

Pleasure
Everything does seem to vie
Which should first attract thine eye:
But since none deserves that grace,
In this crystal view thy face.

Soul
When the Creator's skill is prized,
The rest is all but earth disguised.

Pleasure
Hark how music then prepares
For thy stay these charming airs;
Which the posting winds recall,
40   And suspend the river's fall.

Soul
Had I but any time to lose,
On this I would it all dispose.
Cease tempter. None can chain a mind
Whom this sweet chordage cannot bind.

Chorus
Earth cannot show so brave a sight
As when a single soul does fence
The batteries of alluring sense,
And heaven views it with delight.

Then persevere: for still new charges sound:
50   And if thou overcom'st thou shalt be crowned.

Pleasure
All this fair, and soft, and sweet,
    Which scatteringly doth shine,
Shall within one beauty meet,
    And she be only thine.

Soul
If things of sight such heavens be,
What heavens are those we cannot see?

Pleasure
Wheresoe'er thy foot shall go
    The minted gold shall lie;
Till thou purchase all below,
60   And want new worlds to buy.

Soul
Were't not a price who'd value gold?
And that's worth nought that can be sold.

Pleasure
Wilt thou all the glory have
    That war or peace commend?
Half the world shall be thy slave
    The other half thy friend.

Soul
What friends, if to myself untrue?
What slaves, unless I captive you?

Pleasure
Thou shalt know each hidden cause;
70   And see the future time:
Try what depth the centre draws;
    And then to heaven climb.

Soul
None thither mounts by the degree
Of knowledge, but humility.

Chorus
Triumph, triumph, victorious soul;
The world has not one pleasure more:
The rest does lie beyond the pole,
And is thine everlasting store.

ON A DROP OF DEW

See how the orient dew,
Shed from the bosom of the morn
    Into the blowing roses,
Yet careless of its mansion new;
For the clear region where 'twas born
    Round in itself incloses:
And in its little globe's extent,
Frames as it can its native element.
    How it the purple flower does slight,
10   Scarce touching where it lies,
    But gazing back upon the skies,
      Shines with a mournful light;
        Like its own tear,
Because so long divided from the sphere.
    Restless it rolls and unsecure,
      Trembling lest it grow impure:
    Till the warm sun pity its pain,
And to the skies exhale it back again.
    So the soul, that drop, that ray
20 Of the clear fountain of eternal day,
Could it within the human flower be seen,

Remembering still its former height,
  Shuns the sweet leaves and blossoms green;
And, recollecting its own light,
Does, in its pure and circling thoughts, express
The greater heaven in an heaven less.
  In how coy a figure wound,
  Every way it turns away:
  So the world excluding round,
30 Yet receiving in the day.
  Dark beneath, but bright above:
  Here disdaining, there in love.
How loose and easy hence to go:
How girt and ready to ascend.
Moving but on a point below,
It all about does upwards bend.
Such did the manna's sacred dew distil;
White, and entire, though congealed and chill.
Congealed on earth: but does,dissolving, run
40 Into the glories of the almighty sun.

THE CORONET

When for the thorns with which I long, too long,
  With many a piercing wound,
  My Saviour's head have crowned,
I seek with garlands to redress that wrong:
  Through every garden, every mead,
I gather flowers (my fruits are only flowers)
  Dismantling all the fragrant towers
That once adorned my shepherdess's head.
And now when I have summed up all my store,
10 Thinking (so I myself deceive)
  So rich a chaplet thence to weave
As never yet the King of Glory wore:
  Alas I find the serpent old

That, twining in his speckled breast,
About the flowers disguised does fold,
With wreaths of fame and interest.
Ah, foolish man, that wouldst debase with them,
And mortal glory, heaven's diadem!
But Thou who only couldst the serpent tame,
20   Either his slippery knots at once untie,
And disentangle all his winding snare:
Or shatter too with him my curious frame:
And let these wither, so that he may die,
Though set with skill and chosen out with care.
That they, while Thou on both their spoils dost tread,
May crown thy feet, that could not crown thy head.

EYES AND TEARS

1
How wisely nature did decree,
With the same eyes to weep and see!
That, having viewed the object vain,
They might be ready to complain.

2
And, since the self-deluding sight,
In a false angle takes each height;
These tears which better measure all,
Like watery lines and plummets fall.

3
Two tears, which Sorrow long did weigh
10   Within the scales of either eye,
And then paid out in equal poise,
Are the true price of all my joys.

4

What in the world most fair appears,
Yea even laughter, turns to tears:
And all the jewels which we prize,
Melt in these pendants of the eyes.

5

I have through every garden been,
Amongst the red, the white, the green;
And yet, from all the flowers I saw,
20   No honey, but these tears could draw.

6

So the all-seeing sun each day
Distils the world with chemic ray;
But finds the essence only showers,
Which straight in pity back he pours.

7

Yet happy they whom grief doth bless,
That weep the more, and see the less:
And, to preserve their sight more true,
Bathe still their eyes in their own dew.

8

So Magdalen, in tears more wise
30   Dissolved those captivating eyes,
Whose liquid chains could flowing meet
To fetter her Redeemer's feet.

9

Not full sails hasting loaden home,
Nor the chaste lady's pregnant womb,
Nor Cynthia teeming shows so fair,
As two eyes swollen with weeping are.

10

The sparkling glance that shoots desire,
Drenched in these waves, does lose its fire.
Yea oft the Thunderer pity takes
40   And here the hissing lightning slakes.

11

The incense was to heaven dear,
Not as a perfume, but a tear.
And stars show lovely in the night,
But as they seem the tears of light.

12

Ope then mine eyes your double sluice,
And practise so your noblest use.
For others too can see, or sleep;
But only human eyes can weep.

13

Now like two clouds dissolving, drop,
50   And at each tear in distance stop:
Now like two fountains trickle down;
Now like two floods o'erturn and drown.

14

Thus let your streams o'erflow your springs,
Till eyes and tears be the same things:
And each the other's difference bears;
These weeping eyes, those seeing tears.

BERMUDAS

Where the remote Bermudas ride
In the ocean's bosom unespied,
From a small boat, that rowed along,

The listening winds received this song.
    What should we do but sing his praise
That led us through the watery maze,
Unto an isle so long unknown,
And yet far kinder than our own?
Where he the huge sea-monsters wracks,
10   That lift the deep upon their backs.
He lands us on a grassy stage;
Safe from the storms, and prelate's rage.
He gave us this eternal spring,
Which here enamels everything;
And sends the fowls to us in care,
On daily visits through the air.
He hangs in shades the orange bright,
Like golden lamps in a green night.
And does in the pomegranates close
20   Jewels more rich than Ormus shows.
He makes the figs our mouths to meet;
And throws the melons at our feet.
But apples plants of such a price,
No tree could ever bear them twice.
With cedars, chosen by his hand,
From Lebanon, he stores the land.
And makes the hollow seas, that roar,
Proclaim the ambergris on shore.
He cast (of which we rather boast)
30   The gospel's pearl upon our coast.
And in these rocks for us did frame
A temple, where to sound his name.
Oh let our voice his praise exalt,
Till it arrive at heaven's vault:
Which thence (perhaps) rebounding, may
Echo beyond the Mexique Bay.
Thus sung they, in the English boat,
An holy and a cheerful note,
And all the way, to guide their chime,
40   With falling oars they kept the time.

CLORINDA AND DAMON

C. Damon come drive thy flocks this way.
D. No: 'tis too late they went astray.
C. I have a grassy scutcheon spied,
 Where Flora blazons all her pride.
 The grass I aim to feast thy sheep:
 The flowers I for thy temples keep.
D. Grass withers; and the flowers too fade.
C. Seize the short joys then, ere they vade.
 Seest thou that unfrequented cave?
10 *D*. That den? *C*. Love's shrine. *D*. But virtue's grave.
C. In whose cool bosom we may lie
 Safe from the sun. *D*. not heaven's eye.
C. Near this, a fountain's liquid bell
 Tinkles within the concave shell.
D. Might a soul bathe there and be clean,
 Or slake its drought? *C*. What is't you mean?
D. These once had been enticing things,
 Clorinda, pastures, caves, and springs.
C. And what late change? *D*. The other day
20 Pan met me. *C*. What did great Pan say?
D. Words that transcend poor shepherds' skill,
 But he e'er since my songs does fill:
 And his name swells my slender oat.
C. Sweet must Pan sound in Damon's note.
D. Clorinda's voice might make it sweet.
C. Who would not in Pan's praises meet?

Chorus
Of Pan the flowery pastures sing,
Caves echo, and the fountains ring.
Sing then while he doth us inspire;
30 For all the world is our Pan's choir.

A DIALOGUE BETWEEN THE SOUL AND BODY

Soul
O who shall, from this dungeon, raise
A soul enslaved so many ways?
With bolts of bones, that fettered stands
In feet; and manacled in hands.
Here blinded with an eye; and there
Deaf with the drumming of an ear.
A soul hung up, as 'twere, in chains
Of nerves, and arteries, and veins.
Tortured, besides each other part,
In a vain head, and double heart.

Body
O who shall me deliver whole,
From bonds of this tyrannic soul?
Which, stretched upright, impales me so,
That mine own precipice I go;
And warms and moves this needless frame:
(A fever could but do the same.)
And, wanting where its spite to try,
Has made me live to let me die.
A body that could never rest,
Since this ill spirit it possessed.

Soul
What magic could me thus confine
Within another's grief to pine?
Where whatsoever it complain,
I feel, that cannot feel, the pain.
And all my care itself employs,
That to preserve, which me destroys:
Constrained not only to endure
Diseases, but, what's worse, the cure:
And ready oft the port to gain,
Am shipwrecked into health again.

Body

But physic yet could never reach
The maladies thou me dost teach;
Whom first the cramp of hope dost tear:
And then the palsy shakes of fear.
The pestilence of love does heat:
Or hatred's hidden ulcer eat.
Joy's cheerful madness does perplex:
Or sorrow's other madness vex.
Which knowledge forces me to know;
40   And memory will not forgo.
What but a soul could have the wit
To build me up for sin so fit?
So architects do square and hew,
Green trees that in the forest grew.

THE NYMPH COMPLAINING FOR THE DEATH OF HER FAWN

The wanton troopers riding by
Have shot my fawn and it will die.
Ungentle men! They cannot thrive
To kill thee. Thou ne'er didst alive
Them any harm: alas nor could
Thy death yet do them any good.
I'm sure I never wished them ill;
Nor do I for all this; nor will:
But, if my simple prayers may yet
10   Prevail with heaven to forget
Thy murder, I will join my tears
Rather than fail. But, O my fears!
It cannot die so. Heaven's King
Keeps register of everything:
And nothing may we use in vain.
Even beasts must be with justice slain;

Else men are made their deodands.
Though they should wash their guilty hands
In this warm life-blood, which doth part
20 From thine, and wound me to the heart,
Yet could they not be clean: their stain
Is dyed in such a purple grain.
There is not such another in
The world, to offer for their sin.

Unconstant Sylvio, when yet
I had not found him counterfeit,
One morning (I remember well)
Tied in this silver chain and bell,
Gave it to me: nay and I know
30 What he said then; I'm sure I do.
Said he, look how your huntsman here
Hath taught a fawn to hunt his dear.
But Sylvio soon had me beguiled.
This waxed tame, while he grew wild,
And quite regardless of my smart,
Left me his fawn, but took his heart.

Thenceforth I set myself to play
My solitary time away,
With this: and very well content,
40 Could so mine idle life have spent.
For it was full of sport; and light
Of foot, and heart; and did invite,
Me to its game: it seemed to bless
Itself in me. How could I less
Than love it? O I cannot be
Unkind, to a beast that loveth me.

Had it lived long, I do not know
Whether it too might have done so
As Sylvio did: his gifts might be
50 Perhaps as false or more than he.
But I am sure, for ought that I
Could in so short a time espy,
Thy love was far more better than

The love of false and cruel men.
　　　With sweetest milk, and sugar, first
I it at mine own fingers nursed.
And as it grew, so every day
It waxed more white and sweet than they.
It had so sweet a breath! And oft
60　I blushed to see its foot more soft,
And white, (shall I say than my hand?)
Nay any lady's of the land.
　　　It is a wondrous thing, how fleet
'Twas on those little silver feet.
With what a pretty skipping grace,
It oft would challenge me the race:
And when't had left me far away,
'Twould stay, and run again, and stay.
For it was nimbler much than hinds;
70　And trod, as if on the four winds.
　　　I have a garden of my own,
But so with roses overgrown,
And lilies, that you would it guess
To be a little wilderness.
And all the springtime of the year
It only loved to be there.
Among the beds of lilies, I
Have sought it oft, where it should lie;
Yet could not, till itself would rise,
80　Find it, although before mine eyes.
For, in the flaxen lilies' shade,
It like a bank of lilies laid.
Upon the roses it would feed,
Until its lips even seemed to bleed:
And then to me 'twould boldly trip,
And print those roses on my lip.
But all its chief delight was still
On roses thus itself to fill:
And its pure virgin limbs to fold
90　In whitest sheets of lilies cold.

Had it lived long, it would have been
Lilies without, roses within.
    O help! O help! I see it faint:
And die as calmly as a saint.
See how it weeps. The tears do come
Sad, slowly dropping like a gum.
So weeps the wounded balsam: so
The holy frankincense doth flow.
The brotherless Heliades

100 Melt in such amber tears as these.
    I in a golden vial will
Keep these two crystal tears; and fill
It till it do o'erflow with mine;
Then place it in Diana's shrine.
    Now my sweet fawn is vanished to
Whither the swans and turtles go:
In fair Elysium to endure,
With milk-white lambs, and ermines pure.
O do not run too fast: for I

110 Will but bespeak thy grave, and die.
    First my unhappy statue shall
Be cut in marble; and withal,
Let it be weeping too: but there
The engraver sure his art may spare;
For I so truly thee bemoan,
That I shall weep though I be stone:
Until my tears, still dropping, wear
My breast, themselves engraving there.
There at my feet shalt thou be laid,

120 Of purest alabaster made:
For I would have thine image be
White as I can, though not as thee.

YOUNG LOVE

1

Come little infant, love me now,
    While thine unsuspected years
Clear thine aged father's brow
    From cold jealousy and fears.

2

Pretty surely 'twere to see
    By young love old time beguiled:
While our sportings are as free
    As the nurse's with the child.

3

Common beauties stay fifteen;
    Such as yours should swifter move;
Whose fair blossoms are too green
    Yet for lust, but not for love.

4

Love as much the snowy lamb
    Or the wanton kid does prize,
As the lusty bull or ram,
    For his morning sacrifice.

5

Now then love me: time may take
    Thee before thy time away:
Of this need we'll virtue make,
    And learn love before we may.

6

So we win of doubtful fate;
    And, if good she to us meant,
We that good shall antedate,
    Or, if ill, that ill prevent.

7

Thus as kingdoms, frustrating
   Other titles to their crown,
In the cradle crown their king,
   So all foreign claims to drown,

8

So, to make all rivals vain,
30   Now I crown thee with my love:
Crown me with thy love again,
   And we both shall monarchs prove.

TO HIS COY MISTRESS

Had we but world enough, and time,
This coyness lady were no crime.
We would sit down, and think which way
To walk, and pass our long love's day.
Thou by the Indian Ganges' side
Shouldst rubies find: I by the tide
Of Humber would complain. I would
Love you ten years before the flood:
And you should if you please refuse
10   Till the conversion of the Jews.
My vegetable love should grow
Vaster than empires, and more slow.
An hundred years should go to praise
Thine eyes, and on thy forehead gaze.
Two hundred to adore each breast:
But thirty thousand to the rest.
An age at least to every part,
And the last age should show your heart.
For lady you deserve this state:
20   Nor would I love at lower rate.
   But at my back I always hear

Time's winged chariot hurrying near:
And yonder all before us lie
Deserts of vast eternity.
Thy beauty shall no more be found;
Nor, in thy marble vault, shall sound
My echoing song: then worms shall try
That long preserved virginity:
And your quaint honour turn to dust;
30   And into ashes all my lust.
The grave's a fine and private place,
But none I think do there embrace.
    Now therefore, while the youthful hue
Sits on thy skin like morning dew,
And while thy willing soul transpires
At every pore with instant fires,
Now let us sport us while we may;
And now, like amorous birds of prey,
Rather at once our time devour,
40   Than languish in his slow-chapped power.
Let us roll all our strength, and all
Our sweetness, up into one ball:
And tear our pleasures with rough strife,
Thorough the iron gates of life.
Thus, though we cannot make our sun
Stand still, yet we will make him run.

THE UNFORTUNATE LOVER

1
Alas, how pleasant are their days
With whom the infant love yet plays!
Sorted by pairs, they still are seen
By fountains cool, and shadows green.
But soon these flames do lose their light,
Like meteors of a summer's night:
Nor can they to that region climb,
To make impression upon time.

2

'Twas in a shipwreck, when the seas
10   Ruled, and the winds did what they please,
That my poor lover floating lay,
And, ere brought forth, was cast away:
Till at the last the master-wave
Upon the rock his mother drave;
And there she split against the stone,
In a Caesarian section.

3

The sea him lent these bitter tears
Which at his eyes he always bears.
And from the winds the sighs he bore,
20   Which through his surging breast do roar.
No day he saw but that which breaks,
Through frighted clouds in forked streaks.
While round the rattling thunder hurled,
As at the funeral of the world.

4

While nature to his birth presents
This masque of quarrelling elements;
A numerous fleet of cormorants black,
That sailed insulting o'er the wrack,
Received into their cruel care
30   The unfortunate and abject heir:
Guardians most fit to entertain
The orphan of the hurricane.

5

They fed him up with hopes and air,
Which soon digested to despair.
And as one cormorant fed him, still
Another on his heart did bill.
Thus while they famish him, and feast,
He both consumed, and increased:
And languished with doubtful breath,
40   The amphibium of life and death.

6

And now, when angry heaven would
Behold a spectacle of blood,
Fortune and he are called to play
At sharp before it all the day:
And tyrant love his breast does ply
With all his winged artillery.
Whilst he, betwixt the flames and waves,
Like Ajax, the mad tempest braves.

7

See how he naked and fierce does stand,
Cuffing the thunder with one hand;
While with the other he does lock,
And grapple, with the stubborn rock:
From which he with each wave rebounds,
Torn into flames, and ragged with wounds.
And all he says, a lover dressed
In his own blood does relish best.

8

This is the only banneret
That ever love created yet:
Who though, by the malignant stars,
Forced to live in storms and wars;
Yet dying leaves a perfume here,
And music within every ear:
And he in story only rules,
In a field sable a lover gules.

THE GALLERY

1

Clora come view my soul, and tell
Whether I have contrived it well.
Now all its several lodgings lie
Composed into one gallery;
And the great arras-hangings, made
Of various faces, by are laid;

That, for all furniture, you'll find
Only your picture in my mind.

2

Here thou art painted in the dress
10 Of an inhuman murderess;
Examining upon our hearts
Thy fertile shop of cruel arts:
Engines more keen than ever yet
Adorned tyrant's cabinet;
Of which the most tormenting are
Black eyes, red lips, and curled hair.

3

But, on the other side, thou art drawn
Like to Aurora in the dawn;
When in the east she slumbering lies,
20 And stretches out her milky thighs;
While all the morning choir does sing,
And manna falls, and roses spring;
And, at thy feet, the wooing doves
Sit perfecting their harmless loves.

4

Like an enchantress here thou show'st,
Vexing thy restless lover's ghost;
And, by a light obscure, dost rave
Over his entrails, in the cave;
Divining thence, with horrid care,
30 How long thou shalt continue fair;
And (when informed) them throw'st away,
To be the greedy vulture's prey.

5

But, against that, thou sit'st afloat
Like Venus in her pearly boat.
The halcyons, calming all that's nigh,
Betwixt the air and water fly.
Or, if some rolling wave appears,

A mass of ambergris it bears.
Nor blows more wind than what may well
40   Convoy the perfume to the smell.

6

These pictures and a thousand more,
Of thee, my gallery do store;
In all the forms thou canst invent
Either to please me, or torment:
For thou alone to people me,
Art grown a numerous colony;
And a collection choicer far
Than or Whitehall's, or Mantua's were.

7

But, of these pictures and the rest,
50   That at the entrance likes me best:
Where the same posture, and the look
Remains, with which I first was took.
A tender shepherdess, whose hair
Hangs loosely playing in the air,
Transplanting flowers from the green hill,
To crown her head, and bosom fill.

THE FAIR SINGER

1

To make a final conquest of all me,
Love did compose so sweet an enemy,
In whom both beauties to my death agree,
Joining themselves in fatal harmony;
That while she with her eyes my heart does bind,
She with her voice might captivate my mind.

2

I could have fled from one but singly fair:
My disentangled soul itself might save,
Breaking the curled trammels of her hair.
10   But how should I avoid to be her slave,

Whose subtle art invisibly can wreathe
My fetters of the very air I breathe?

3

It had been easy fighting in some plain,
Where victory might hang in equal choice,
But all resistance against her is vain,
Who has the advantage both of eyes and voice,
And all my forces needs must be undone,
She having gained both the wind and sun.

MOURNING

1

You, that decipher out the fate
Of human offsprings from the skies,
What mean these infants which of late
Spring from the stars of Chlora's eyes?

2

Her eyes confused, and doubled o'er,
With tears suspended ere they flow;
Seem bending upwards, to restore
To heaven, whence it came, their woe.

3

When, moulding of the watery spheres,
10 Slow drops untie themselves away;
As if she, with those precious tears,
Would strow the ground where Strephon lay.

4

Yet some affirm, pretending art,
Her eyes have so her bosom drowned,
Only to soften near her heart
A place to fix another wound.

5

And, while vain pomp does her restrain
Within her solitary bower,

She courts herself in amorous rain;
20   Herself both Danae and the shower.

6

Nay others, bolder, hence esteem
Joy now so much her master grown,
That whatsoever does but seem
Like grief, is from her windows thrown.

7

Nor that she pays, while she survives,
To her dead love this tribute due;
But casts abroad these donatives,
At the installing of a new.

8

How wide they dream! The Indian slaves
30   That sink for pearl through seas profound,
Would find her tears yet deeper waves
And not of one the bottom sound.

9

I yet my silent judgment keep,
Disputing not what they believe:
But sure as oft as women weep,
It is to be supposed they grieve.

DAPHNIS AND CHLOE

1

Daphnis must from Chloe part:
Now is come the dismal hour
That must all his hopes devour,
All his labour, all his art.

2

Nature, her own sex's foe,
Long had taught her to be coy:
But she neither knew to enjoy,
Nor yet let her lover go.

3

But, with this sad news surprised,
Soon she let that niceness fall;
And would gladly yield to all,
So it had his stay comprised.

4

Nature so herself does use
To lay by her wonted state,
Lest the world should separate;
Sudden parting closer glues.

5

He, well-read in all the ways
By which men their siege maintain,
Knew not that the fort to gain
Better 'twas the siege to raise.

6

But he came so full possessed
With the grief of parting thence,
That he had not so much sense
As to see he might be blessed.

7

Till Love in her language breathed
Words she never spake before;
But than legacies no more
To a dying man bequeathed.

8

For, alas, the time was spent,
Now the latest minute's run
When poor Daphnis is undone,
Between joy and sorrow rent.

9

At that *Why*, that *Stay my Dear*,
His disordered locks he tare;

And with rolling eyes did glare,
And his cruel fate forswear.

10

As the soul of one scarce dead,
With the shrieks of friends aghast,
Looks distracted back in haste,
40   And then straight again is fled.

11

So did wretched Daphnis look,
Frighting her he loved most.
At the last, this lover's ghost
Thus his leave resolved took.

12

Are my hell and heaven joined
More to torture him that dies?
Could departure not suffice,
But that you must then grow kind?

13

Ah my Chloe how have I
50   Such a wretched minute found,
When thy favours should me wound
More than all thy cruelty?

14

So to the condemned wight
The delicious cup we fill;
And allow him all he will,
For his last and short delight.

15

But I will not now begin
Such a debt unto my foe;
Nor to my departure owe
60   What my presence could not win.

16

Absence is too much alone:
Better 'tis to go in peace,
Than my losses to increase
By a late fruition.

17

Why should I enrich my fate?
'Tis a vanity to wear,
For my executioner,
Jewels of so high a rate.

18

Rather I away will pine
In a manly stubbornness
Than be fatted up express
For the cannibal to dine

19

Whilst this grief does thee disarm,
All the enjoyment of our love
But the ravishment would prove
Of a body dead while warm.

20

And I parting should appear
Like the gourmand Hebrew dead,
While with quails and manna fed,
He does through the desert err.

21

Or the witch that midnight wakes
For the fern, whose magic weed
In one minute casts the seed,
And invisible him makes.

22

Gentler times for love are meant.
Who for parting pleasure strain

Gather roses in the rain,
Wet themselves and spoil their scent.

23
Farewell therefore all the fruit
90 Which I could from love receive:
Joy will not with sorrow weave,
Nor will I this grief pollute.

24
Fate I come, as dark, as sad,
As thy malice could desire;
Yet bring with me all the fire
That Love in his torches had.

25
At these words away he broke;
As who long has praying lien,
To his headsman makes the sign,
100 And receives the parting stroke.

26
But hence virgins all beware.
Last night he with Phlogis slept;
This night for Dorinda kept;
And but rid to take the air.

27
Yet he does himself excuse;
Nor indeed without a cause.
For, according to the laws,
Why did Chloe once refuse?

THE DEFINITION OF LOVE

1
My love is of a birth as rare
As 'tis for object strange and high:
It was begotten by Despair
Upon Impossibility.

2

Magnanimous Despair alone
Could show me so divine a thing,
Where feeble Hope could ne'er have flown
But vainly flapped its tinsel wing.

3

And yet I quickly might arrive
10 Where my extended soul is fixed,
But Fate does iron wedges drive,
And always crowds itself betwixt.

4

For Fate with jealous eye does see
Two perfect loves; nor lets them close:
Their union would her ruin be,
And her tyrannic power depose.

5

And therefore her decrees of steel
Us as the distant poles have placed,
(Though Love's whole world on us doth wheel)
20 Not by themselves to be embraced.

6

Unless the giddy heaven fall,
And earth some new convulsion tear;
And, us to join, the world should all
Be cramped into a planisphere.

7

As lines so loves oblique may well
Themselves in every angle greet:
But ours so truly parallel,
Though infinite can never meet.

8

Therefore the love which us doth bind,
30 But Fate so enviously debars,
Is the conjunction of the mind,
And opposition of the stars.

THE PICTURE OF LITTLE T. C.
IN A PROSPECT OF FLOWERS

1

See with what simplicity
This nymph begins her golden days!
In the green grass she loves to lie,
And there with her fair aspect tames
The wilder flowers, and gives them names:
But only with the roses plays;
               And them does tell
What colour best becomes them, and what smell.

2

Who can foretell for what high cause
This darling of the Gods was born!
Yet this is she whose chaster laws
The wanton Love shall one day fear,
And, under her command severe,
See his bow broke and ensigns torn.
               Happy, who can
Appease this virtuous enemy of man!

3

O then let me in time compound,
And parley with those conquering eyes;
Ere they have tried their force to wound,
Ere, with their glancing wheels, they drive
In triumph over hearts that strive,
And them that yield but more despise.
               Let me be laid,
Where I may see thy glories from some shade.

4

Meantime, whilst every verdant thing
Itself does at thy beauty charm,
Reform the errors of the spring;
Make that the tulips may have share
Of sweetness, seeing they are fair;

30   And roses of their thorns disarm:
                          But most procure
    That violets may a longer age endure.

5

But O young beauty of the woods,
Whom nature courts with fruits and flowers,
Gather the flowers, but spare the buds;
Lest Flora angry at thy crime,
To kill her infants in their prime,
Do quickly make the example yours;
                     And, ere we see,
40   Nip in the blossom all our hopes and thee.

THE MATCH

1

Nature had long a treasure made
    Of all her choicest store;
Fearing, when she should be decayed,
    To beg in vain for more.

2

Her orientest colours there,
    And essences most pure,
With sweetest perfumes hoarded were,
    All as she thought secure.

3

She seldom them unlocked, or used,
10   But with the nicest care;
For, with one grain of them diffused,
    She could the world repair.

4

But likeness soon together drew
    What she did separate lay;
Of which one perfect beauty grew,
    And that was Celia.

5

Love wisely had of long foreseen
   That he must once grow old;
And therefore stored a magazine,
20   To save him from the cold.

6

He kept the several cells replete
   With nitre thrice refined;
The naphtha's and the sulphur's heat,
   And all that burns the mind.

7

He fortified the double gate,
   And rarely thither came;
For, with one spark of these, he straight
   All nature could inflame.

8

Till, by vicinity so long,
30   A nearer way they sought;
And, grown magnetically strong,
   Into each other wrought.

9

Thus all his fuel did unite
   To make one fire high:
None ever burned so hot, so bright;
   And Celia that am I.

10

So we alone the happy rest,
   Whilst all the world is poor,
And have within ourselves possessed
40   All love's and nature's store.

THE MOWER AGAINST GARDENS

Luxurious man, to bring his vice in use,
   Did after him the world seduce:
And from the fields the flowers and plants allure,

Where nature was most plain and pure.
He first enclosed within the gardens square
    A dead and standing pool of air:
And a more luscious earth for them did knead,
    Which stupified them while it fed.
The pink grew then as double as his mind;
10   The nutriment did change the kind.
With strange perfumes he did the roses taint.
    And flowers themselves were taught to paint.
The tulip, white, did for complexion seek;
    And learned to interline its cheek:
Its onion root they then so high did hold,
    That one was for a meadow sold.
Another world was searched, through oceans new,
    To find the Marvel of Peru.
And yet these rarities might be allowed,
20   To man, that sovereign thing and proud;
Had he not dealt between the bark and tree,
    Forbidden mixtures there to see.
No plant now knew the stock from which it came;
    He grafts upon the wild the tame:
That the uncertain and adulterate fruit
    Might put the palate in dispute.
His green seraglio has its eunuchs too;
    Lest any tyrant him outdo.
And in the cherry he does nature vex,
30   To procreate without a sex.
'Tis all enforced; the fountain and the grot;
    While the sweet fields do lie forgot:
Where willing nature does to all dispense
    A wild and fragrant innocence:
And fauns and fairies do the meadows till,
    More by their presence than their skill.
Their statues polished by some ancient hand,
    May to adorn the gardens stand:
But howsoe'er the figures do excel,
40   The gods themselves with us do dwell.

DAMON THE MOWER

1

Hark how the mower Damon sung,
With love of Juliana stung!
While everything did seem to paint
The scene more fit for his complaint.
Like her fair eyes the day was fair;
But scorching like his amorous care.
Sharp like his scythe his sorrow was,
And withered like his hopes the grass.

2

Oh what unusual heats are here,
Which thus our sunburned meadows sear!
The grasshopper its pipe gives o'er;
And hamstringed frogs can dance no more.
But in the brook the green frog wades;
And grasshoppers seek out the shades.
Only the snake, that kept within,
Now glitters in its second skin.

3

This heat the sun could never raise,
Nor dog-star so inflames the days.
It from a higher beauty grow'th,
Which burns the fields and mower both:
Which made the dog, and makes the sun
Hotter than his own Phaeton.
Not July causeth these extremes,
But Juliana's scorching beams.

4

Tell me where I may pass the fires
Of the hot day, or hot desires.
To what cool cave shall I descend,
Or to what gelid fountain bend?

Alas! I look for ease in vain,
30 When remedies themselves complain.
No moisture but my tears do rest,
Nor cold but in her icy breast.

5

How long wilt thou, fair shepherdess,
Esteem me, and my presents less?
To thee the harmless snake I bring,
Disarmed of its teeth and sting.
To thee chameleons changing hue,
And oak leaves tipped with honey dew.
Yet thou ungrateful hast not sought
40 Nor what they are, nor who them brought.

6

I am the mower Damon, known
Through all the meadows I have mown.
On me the morn her dew distils
Before her darling daffodils.
And, if at noon my toil me heat,
The sun himself licks off my sweat.
While, going home, the evening sweet
In cowslip-water bathes my feet.

7

What, though the piping shepherd stock
50 The plains with an unnumbered flock,
This scythe of mine discovers wide
More ground than all his sheep do hide.
With this the golden fleece I shear
Of all these closes every year.
And though in wool more poor than they,
Yet am I richer far in hay.

8

Nor am I so deformed to sight,
If in my scythe I looked right;
In which I see my picture done,
60   As in a crescent moon the sun.
The deathless fairies take me oft
To lead them in their dances soft;
And, when I tune myself to sing,
About me they contract their ring.

9

How happy might I still have mowed,
Had not Love here his thistles sowed!
But now I all the day complain,
Joining my labour to my pain;
And with my scythe cut down the grass,
70   Yet still my grief is where it was:
But, when the iron blunter grows,
Sighing I whet my scythe and woes.

10

While thus he threw his elbow round,
Depopulating all the ground,
And, with his whistling scythe, does cut
Each stroke between the earth and root,
The edged steel by careless chance
Did into his own ankle glance;
And there among the grass fell down,
80   By his own scythe, the mower mown.

11

Alas! said he, these hurts are slight
To those that die by love's despite.
With shepherd's purse, and clown's all-heal,
The blood I stanch, and wound I seal.
Only for him no cure is found,
Whom Juliana's eyes do wound.

'Tis death alone that this must do:
For Death thou art a mower too.

THE MOWER TO THE GLOW-WORMS

1
Ye living lamps, by whose dear light
The nightingale does sit so late,
And studying all the summer night,
Her matchless songs does meditate;

2
Ye country comets, that portend
No war, nor prince's funeral,
Shining unto no higher end
Than to presage the grass's fall;

3
Ye glow-worms, whose officious flame
10 To wandering mowers shows the way,
That in the night have lost their aim,
And after foolish fires do stray;

4
Your courteous lights in vain you waste,
Since Juliana here is come,
For she my mind hath so displaced
That I shall never find my home.

THE MOWER'S SONG

1

My mind was once the true survey
Of all these meadows fresh and gay;
And in the greenness of the grass
Did see its hopes as in a glass;
When Juliana came, and she
What I do to the grass, does to my thoughts and me.

2

But these, while I with sorrow pine,
Grew more luxuriant still and fine;
That not one blade of grass you spied,
But had a flower on either side;
When Juliana came, and she
What I do to the grass, does to my thoughts and me.

3

Unthankful meadows, could you so
A fellowship so true forgo,
And in your gaudy May-games meet,
While I lay trodden under feet?
When Juliana came, and she
What I do to the grass, does to my thoughts and me.

4

But what you in compassion ought,
Shall now by my revenge be wrought:
And flowers, and grass, and I and all,
Will in one common ruin fall.
For Juliana comes, and she
What I do to the grass, does to my thoughts and me.

5

And thus, ye meadows, which have been
Companions of my thoughts more green,

Shall now the heraldry become
With which I shall adorn my tomb;
For Juliana comes, and she
30 What I do to the grass, does to my thoughts and me.

AMETAS AND THESTYLIS MAKING HAY-ROPES

1 / *Ametas*
Think'st thou that this love can stand,
Whilst thou still dost say me nay?
Love unpaid does soon disband:
Love binds love as hay binds hay.

2 / *Thestylis*
Think'st thou that this rope would twine
If we both should turn one way?
Where both parties so combine,
Neither love will twist nor hay.

3 / *Ametas*
Thus you vain excuses find,
10 Which yourself and us delay:
And love ties a woman's mind
Looser than with ropes of hay.

4 / *Thestylis*
What you cannot constant hope
Must be taken as you may.

5 / *Ametas*
Then let's both lay by our rope,
And go kiss within the hay.

MUSIC'S EMPIRE

1

First was the world as one great cymbal made,
Where jarring winds to infant nature played.
All music was a solitary sound,
To hollow rocks and murmuring fountains bound.

2

Jubal first made the wilder notes agree;
And Jubal tuned music's jubilee:
He called the echoes from their sullen cell,
And built the organ's city where they dwell.

3

Each sought a consort in that lovely place;
And virgin trebles wed the manly bass.
From whence the progeny of numbers new
Into harmonious colonies withdrew.

4

Some to the lute, some to the viol went,
And others chose the cornet eloquent.
These practising the wind, and those the wire,
To sing men's triumphs, or in heaven's choir.

5

Then music, the mosaic of the air,
Did of all these a solemn noise prepare:
With which she gained the empire of the ear,
Including all between the earth and sphere.

6

Victorious sounds! yet here your homage do
Unto a gentler conqueror than you;
Who though he flies the music of his praise,
Would with you heaven's hallelujahs raise.

THE GARDEN

1

How vainly men themselves amaze
To win the palm, the oak, or bays;
And their uncessant labours see
Crowned from some single herb or tree.
Whose short and narrow verged shade
Does prudently their toils upbraid;
While all flowers and all trees do close
To weave the garlands of repose.

2

Fair quiet, have I found thee here,
And innocence thy sister dear!
Mistaken long, I sought you then
In busy companies of men.
Your sacred plants, if here below,
Only among the plants will grow.
Society is all but rude,
To this delicious solitude.

3

No white nor red was ever seen
So amorous as this lovely green.
Fond lovers, cruel as their flame,
Cut in these trees their mistress' name.
Little, alas, they know, or heed,
How far these beauties hers exceed!
Fair trees! wheresoe'er your barks I wound,
No name shall but your own be found.

4

When we have run our passion's heat,
Love hither makes his best retreat.
The gods, that mortal beauty chase,
Still in a tree did end their race.

Apollo hunted Daphne so,
30   Only that she might laurel grow.
And Pan did after Syrinx speed,
Not as a nymph, but for a reed.

5

What wondrous life in this I lead!
Ripe apples drop about my head;
The luscious clusters of the vine
Upon my mouth do crush their wine;
The nectarine, and curious peach,
Into my hands themselves do reach;
Stumbling on melons, as I pass,
40   Ensnared with flowers, I fall on grass.

6

Meanwhile the mind, from pleasure less,
Withdraws into its happiness:
The mind, that ocean where each kind
Does straight its own resemblance find;
Yet it creates, transcending these,
Far other worlds, and other seas;
Annihilating all that's made
To a green thought in a green shade.

7

Here at the fountain's sliding foot,
50   Or at some fruit-tree's mossy root,
Casting the body's vest aside,
My soul into the boughs does glide:
There like a bird it sits, and sings,
Then whets, and combs its silver wings;
And, till prepared for longer flight,
Waves in its plumes the various light.

8

Such was that happy garden-state,
While man there walked without a mate:
After a place so pure, and sweet,
60   What other help could yet be meet!
But 'twas beyond a mortal's share
To wander solitary there:
Two paradises 'twere in one
To live in paradise alone.

9

How well the skilful gardener drew
Of flowers and herbs this dial new;
Where from above the milder sun
Does through a fragrant zodiac run;
And, as it works, the industrious bee
70   Computes its time as well as we.
How could such sweet and wholesome hours
Be reckoned but with herbs and flowers!

UPON THE HILL AND GROVE AT BILBROUGH

To the Lord Fairfax

1

See how the arched earth does here
Rise in a perfect hemisphere!
The stiffest compass could not strike
A line more circular and like;
Nor softest pencil draw a brow
So equal as this hill does bow.
It seems as for a model laid,
And that the world by it was made.

2

Here learn ye mountains more unjust,
10 Which to abrupter greatness thrust,
That do with your hook-shouldered height
The earth deform and heaven fright,
For whose excrescence ill-designed,
Nature must a new centre find,
Learn here those humble steps to tread,
Which to securer glory lead.

3

See what a soft access and wide
Lies open to its grassy side;
Nor with the rugged path deters
20 The feet of breathless travellers.
See then how courteous it ascends,
And all the way it rises bends;
Nor for itself the height does gain,
But only strives to raise the plain.

4

Yet thus it all the field commands,
And in unenvied greatness stands,
Discerning further than the cliff
Of heaven-daring Tenerife.
How glad the weary seamen haste
30 When they salute it from the mast!
By night the Northern Star their way
Directs, and this no less by day.

5

Upon its crest this mountain grave
A plump of aged trees does wave.
No hostile hand durst ere invade
With impious steel the sacred shade.
For something always did appear
Of the great Master's terror there:

And men could hear his armour still
40   Rattling through all the grove and hill.

6

Fear of the Master, and respect
Of the great Nymph did it protect;
Vera the Nymph that him inspired,
To whom he often here retired,
And on these oaks engraved her name;
Such wounds alone these woods became:
But ere he well the barks could part
'Twas writ already in their heart.

7

For they ('tis credible) have sense,
50   As we, of love and reverence,
And underneath the coarser rind
The genius of the house do bind.
Hence they successes seem to know,
And in their Lord's advancement grow;
But in no memory were seen
As under this so straight and green.

8

Yet now no further strive to shoot,
Contented if they fix their root.
Nor to the wind's uncertain gust,
60   Their prudent heads too far intrust.
Only sometimes a fluttering breeze
Discourses with the breathing trees;
Which in their modest whispers name
Those acts that swelled the cheek of fame.

9

Much other groves, say they, than these
And other hills him once did please.
Through groves of pikes he thundered then,

And mountains raised of dying men.
For all the civic garlands due
70   To him our branches are but few.
Nor are our trunks enow to bear
The trophies of one fertile year.

10

'Tis true, ye trees nor ever spoke
More certain oracles in oak.
But peace (if you his favour prize)
That courage its own praises flies.
Therefore to your obscurer seats
From his own brightness he retreats:
Nor he the hills without the groves,
80   Nor height but with retirement loves.

UPON APPLETON HOUSE, TO MY LORD FAIRFAX

1

Within this sober frame expect
Work of no foreign architect;
That unto caves the quarries drew,
And forests did to pastures hew;
Who of his great design in pain
Did for a model vault his brain,
Whose columns should so high be raised
To arch the brows that on them gazed.

2

Why should of all things man unruled
10   Such unproportioned dwellings build?
The beasts are by their dens expressed:
And birds contrive an equal nest;
The low-roofed tortoises do dwell
In cases fit of tortoise-shell:

No creature loves an empty space;
Their bodies measure out their place.

3

But he, superfluously spread,
Demands more room alive than dead.
And in his hollow palace goes
20 Where winds as he themselves may lose.
What need of all this marble crust
To impark the wanton mote of dust,
That thinks by breadth the world t'unite
Though the first builders failed in height?

4

But all things are composed here
Like nature, orderly and near:
In which we the dimensions find
Of that more sober age and mind,
When larger sized men did stoop
30 To enter at a narrow loop;
As practising, in doors so strait,
To strain themselves through heaven's gate.

5

And surely when the after age
Shall hither come in pilgrimage,
These sacred places to adore,
By Vere and Fairfax trod before,
Men will dispute how their extent
Within such dwarfish confines went:
And some will smile at this, as well
40 As Romulus his bee-like cell.

6

Humility alone designs
Those short but admirable lines,
By which, ungirt and unconstrained,

Things greater are in less contained.
Let others vainly strive to immure
The circle in the quadrature!
These holy mathematics can
In every figure equal man.

7

Yet thus the laden house does sweat,
50   And scarce endures the Master great:
But where he comes the swelling hall
Stirs, and the square grows spherical;
More by his magnitude distressed,
Than he is by its straitness pressed:
And too officiously it slights
That in itself which him delights.

8

So honour better lowness bears,
Than that unwonted greatness wears.
Height with a certain grace does bend,
60   But low things clownishly ascend.
And yet what needs there here excuse,
Where everything does answer use?
Where neatness nothing can condemn,
Nor pride invent what to contemn?

9

A stately frontispiece of poor
Adorns without the open door:
Nor less the rooms within commends
Daily new furniture of friends.
The house was built upon the place
70   Only as for a mark of grace;
And for an inn to entertain
Its Lord a while, but not remain.

10

Him Bishop's Hill, or Denton may,
Or Bilbrough, better hold than they:
But Nature here hath been so free
As if she said leave this to me.
Art would more neatly have defaced
What she had laid so sweetly waste;
In fragrant gardens, shady woods,
80   Deep meadows, and transparent floods.

11

While with slow eyes we these survey,
And on each pleasant footstep stay,
We opportunely may relate
The progress of this house's fate.
A nunnery first gave it birth.
For virgin buildings oft brought forth.
And all that neighbour-ruin shows
The quarries whence this dwelling rose.

12

Near to this gloomy cloister's gates
90   There dwelt the blooming virgin Thwaites;
Fair beyond measure, and an heir
Which might deformity make fair.
And oft she spent the summer suns
Discoursing with the subtle nuns.
Whence in these words one to her weaved,
(As 'twere by chance) thoughts long conceived.

13

'Within this holy leisure we
'Live innocently as you see.
'These walls restrain the world without,
100   'But hedge our liberty about.
'These bars inclose that wider den
'Of those wild creatures, called men.

'The cloister outward shuts its gates,
'And, from us, locks on them the grates.

14
'Here we, in shining armour white,
'Like virgin Amazons do fight.
'And our chaste lamps we hourly trim,
'Lest the great Bridegroom find them dim.
'Our orient breaths perfumed are
110 'With incense of incessant prayer.
'And holy-water of our tears
'Most strangely our complexion clears.

15
'Not tears of grief; but such as those
'With which calm pleasure overflows;
'Or pity, when we look on you
'That live without this happy vow.
'How should we grieve that must be seen
'Each one a spouse, and each a queen;
'And can in heaven hence behold
120 'Our brighter robes and crowns of gold?

16
'When we have prayed all our beads,
'Someone the holy legend reads;
'While all the rest with needles paint
'The face and graces of the saint.
'But what the linen can't receive
'They in their lives do interweave.
'This work the saints best represents;
'That serves for altar's ornaments.

17
'But much it to our work would add
130 'If here your hand, your face we had:
'By it we would Our Lady touch;

'Yet thus She you resembles much.
'Some of your features, as we sewed,
'Through every shrine should be bestowed.
'And in one beauty we would take
'Enough a thousand saints to make.

18
'And (for I dare not quench the fire
'That me does for your good inspire)
''Twere sacrilege a man to admit
140   'To holy things, for heaven fit.
'I see the angels in a crown
'On you the lilies showering down:
'And round about you glory breaks,
'That something more than human speaks.

19
'All beauty, when at such a height,
'Is so already consecrate.
'Fairfax I know; and long ere this
'Have marked the youth, and what he is.
'But can he such a rival seem
150   'For whom you heaven should disesteem?
'Ah, no! and 'twould more honour prove
'He your *devoto* were, than love.

20
'Here live beloved, and obeyed:
'Each one your sister, each your maid.
'And, if our rule seem strictly penned,
'The rule itself to you shall bend.
'Our abbess too, now far in age,
'Doth your succession near presage.
'How soft the yoke on us would lie,
160   'Might such fair hands as yours it tie!

21

'Your voice, the sweetest of the choir,
'Shall draw heaven nearer, raise us higher.
'And your example, if our head,
'Will soon us to perfection lead.
'Those virtues to us all so dear,
'Will straight grow sanctity when here:
'And that, once sprung, increase so fast
'Till miracles it work at last.

22

'Nor is our order yet so nice,
170 'Delight to banish as a vice.
'Here pleasure piety doth meet;
'One perfecting the other sweet.
'So through the mortal fruit we boil
'The sugar's uncorrupting oil:
'And that which perished while we pull,
'Is thus preserved clear and full.

23

'For such indeed are all our arts;
'Still handling nature's finest parts.
'Flowers dress the altars; for the clothes,
180 'The sea-born amber we compose;
'Balms for the grieved we draw; and pastes
'We mould, as baits for curious tastes.
'What need is here of man? unless
'These as sweet sins we should confess.

24

'Each night among us to your side
'Appoint a fresh and virgin bride;
'Whom if our Lord at midnight find,
'Yet neither should be left behind.
'Where you may lie as chaste in bed,
190 'As pearls together billeted.

'All night embracing arm in arm,
'Like crystal pure with cotton warm.

25
'But what is this to all the store
'Of joys you see, and may make more!
'Try but a while, if you be wise:
'The trial neither costs, nor ties.
Now Fairfax seek her promised faith:
Religion that dispensed hath;
Which she henceforward does begin;
200 The nun's smooth tongue has sucked her in.

26
Oft, though he knew it was in vain,
Yet would he valiantly complain.
'Is this that sanctity so great,
'An art by which you finelier cheat?
'Hypocrite witches, hence avaunt,
'Who though in prison yet enchant!
'Death only can such thieves make fast,
'As rob though in the dungeon cast.

27
'Were there but, when this house was made,
210 'One stone that a just hand had laid,
'It must have fallen upon her head
'Who first thee from thy faith misled.
'And yet, how well soever meant,
'With them 'twould soon grow fraudulent:
'For like themselves they alter all,
'And vice infects the very wall.

28
'But sure those buildings last not long,
'Founded by folly, kept by wrong.
'I know what fruit their gardens yield,

220 'When they it think by night concealed.
'Fly from their vices. 'Tis thy state,
'Not thee, that they would consecrate.
'Fly from their ruin. How I fear
'Though guiltless lest thou perish there.

29

What should he do? He would respect
Religion, but not right neglect:
For first religion taught him right,
And dazzled not but cleared his sight.
Sometimes resolved his sword he draws,
230 But reverenceth then the laws:
For justice still that courage led;
First from a judge, then soldier bred.

30

Small honour would be in the storm.
The court him grants the lawful form;
Which licensed either peace or force,
To hinder the unjust divorce.
Yet still the nuns his right debarred,
Standing upon their holy guard.
Ill-counselled women, do you know
240 Whom you resist, or what you do?

31

Is not this he whose offspring fierce
Shall fight through all the universe;
And with successive valour try
France, Poland, either Germany;
Till one, as long since prophesied,
His horse through conquered Britain ride?
Yet, against fate, his spouse they kept;
And the great race would intercept.

32

Some to the breach against their foes
250   Their wooden saints in vain oppose.
Another bolder stands at push
With their old holy-water brush.
While the disjointed abbess threads
The jingling chain-shot of her beads.
But their loudest cannon were their lungs;
And sharpest weapons were their tongues.

33

But, waving these aside like flies,
Young Fairfax through the wall does rise.
Then the unfrequented vault appeared,
260   And superstitions vainly feared.
The relics false were set to view;
Only the jewels there were true.
But truly bright and holy Thwaites
That weeping at the altar waits.

34

But the glad youth away her bears,
And to the nuns bequeaths her tears:
Who guiltily their prize bemoan,
Like gypsies that a child hath stolen.
Thenceforth (as when the enchantment ends
270   The castle vanishes or rends)
The wasting cloister with the rest
Was in one instant dispossessed.

35

At the demolishing, this seat
To Fairfax fell as by escheat.
And what both nuns and founders willed
'Tis likely better thus fulfilled.
For if the virgin proved not theirs,
The cloister yet remained hers.

Though many a nun there made her vow,
280 'Twas no religious house till now.

36
From that blest bed the hero came,
Whom France and Poland yet does fame:
Who, when retired here to peace,
His warlike studies could not cease;
But laid these gardens out in sport
In the just figure of a fort;
And with five bastions it did fence,
As aiming one for every sense.

37
When in the east the morning ray
290 Hangs out the colours of the day,
The bee through these known alleys hums,
Beating the *dian* with its drums.
Then flowers their drowsy eyelids raise,
Their silken ensigns each displays,
And dries its pan yet dank with dew,
And fills its flask with odours new.

38
These, as their Governor goes by,
In fragrant volleys they let fly;
And to salute their Governess
300 Again as great a charge they press:
None for the virgin Nymph; for she
Seems with the flowers a flower to be.
And think so still! though not compare
With breath so sweet, or cheek so fair.

39
Well shot ye firemen! Oh how sweet,
And round your equal fires do meet;
Whose shrill report no ear can tell,

But echoes to the eye and smell.
See how the flowers, as at parade,
310 Under their colours stand displayed:
Each regiment in order grows,
That of the tulip pink and rose.

40

But when the vigilant patrol
Of stars walks round about the pole,
Their leaves, that to the stalks are curled,
Seem to their staves the ensigns furled.
Then in some flower's beloved hut
Each bee as sentinel is shut;
And sleeps so too: but, if once stirred,
320 She runs you through, or asks the word.

41

Oh thou, that dear and happy isle
The garden of the world erewhile,
Thou paradise of four seas,
Which heaven planted us to please,
But, to exclude the world, did guard
With watery if not flaming sword;
What luckless apple did we taste,
To make us mortal, and thee waste?

42

Unhappy! shall we never more
330 That sweet militia restore,
When gardens only had their towers,
And all the garrisons were flowers,
When roses only arms might bear,
And men did rosy garlands wear?
Tulips, in several colours barred,
Were then the Switzers of our Guard.

43

The gardener had the soldier's place,
And his more gentle forts did trace.
The nursery of all things green
340 Was then the only magazine.
The winter quarters were the stoves,
Where he the tender plants removes.
But war all this doth overgrow:
We ordnance plant and powder sow.

44

And yet there walks one on the sod
Who, had it pleased him and God,
Might once have made our gardens spring
Fresh as his own and flourishing.
But he preferred to the Cinque Ports
350 These five imaginary forts:
And, in those half-dry trenches, spanned
Power which the ocean might command.

45

For he did, with his utmost skill,
Ambition weed, but conscience till.
Conscience, that heaven-nursed plant,
Which most our earthly gardens want.
A prickling leaf it bears, and such
As that which shrinks at every touch;
But flowers eternal, and divine,
360 That in the crowns of saints do shine.

46

The sight does from these bastions ply,
The invisible artillery;
And at proud Cawood Castle seems
To point the battery of its beams.
As if it quarrelled in the seat
The ambition of its prelate great.

But o'er the meads below it plays,
Or innocently seems to gaze.

47

And now to the abyss I pass
370   Of that unfathomable grass,
Where men like grasshoppers appear,
But grasshoppers are giants there:
They, in their squeaking laugh, contemn
Us as we walk more low than them:
And, from the precipices tall
Of the green spires, to us do call.

48

To see men through this meadow dive,
We wonder how they rise alive.
As, under water, none does know
380   Whether he fall through it or go.
But, as the mariners that sound,
And show upon their lead the ground,
They bring up flowers so to be seen,
And prove they've at the bottom been.

49

No scene that turns with engines strange
Does oftener than these meadows change.
For when the sun the grass hath vexed,
The tawny mowers enter next;
Who seem like Israelites to be,
390   Walking on foot through a green sea.
To them the grassy deeps divide,
And crowd a lane to either side.

50

With whistling scythe, and elbow strong,
These massacre the grass along:
While one, unknowing, carves the rail,

Whose yet unfeathered quills her fail.
The edge all bloody from its breast
He draws, and does his stroke detest;
Fearing the flesh untimely mowed
400   To him a fate as black forebode.

51

But bloody Thestylis, that waits
To bring the mowing camp their cates,
Greedy as kites has trussed it up,
And forthwith means on it to sup:
When on another quick she lights,
And cries, he called us Israelites;
But now, to make his saying true,
Rails rain for quails, for manna dew.

52

Unhappy birds! what does it boot
410   To build below the grass's root;
When lowness is unsafe as height,
And chance o'ertakes what scapeth spite?
And now your orphan parents' call
Sounds your untimely funeral.
Death-trumpets creak in such a note,
And 'tis the sourdine in their throat.

53

Or sooner hatch or higher build:
The mower now commands the field;
In whose new traverse seemeth wrought
420   A camp of battle newly fought:
Where, as the meads with hay, the plain
Lies quilted o'er with bodies slain:
The women that with forks it fling,
Do represent the pillaging.

54

And now the careless victors play,
Dancing the triumphs of the hay;
Where every mower's wholesome heat
Smells like an Alexander's sweat.
Their females fragrant as the mead
430 Which they in fairy circles tread:
When at their dance's end they kiss,
Their new-made hay not sweeter is.

55

When after this 'tis piled in cocks,
Like a calm sea it shows the rocks:
We wondering in the river near
How boats among them safely steer.
Or, like the desert Memphis sand,
Short pyramids of hay do stand.
And such the Roman camps do rise
440 In hills for soldiers' obsequies.

56

This scene again withdrawing brings
A new and empty face of things;
A levelled space, as smooth and plain,
As cloths for Lely stretched to stain.
The world when first created sure
Was such a table rase and pure.
Or rather such is the *toril*
Ere the bulls enter at Madril.

57

For to this naked equal flat,
450 Which Levellers take pattern at,
The villagers in common chase
Their cattle, which it closer rase;
And what below the scythe increased
Is pinched yet nearer by the beast.

Such, in the painted world, appeared
Davenant with th'universal herd.

58
They seem within the polished grass
A landskip drawn in looking-glass.
And shrunk in the huge pasture show
460 As spots, so shaped, on faces do.
Such fleas, ere they approach the eye,
In multiplying glasses lie.
They feed so wide, so slowly move,
As constellations do above.

59
Then, to conclude these pleasant acts,
Denton sets ope its cataracts;
And makes the meadow truly be
(What it but seemed before) a sea.
For, jealous of its Lord's long stay,
470 It tries to invite him thus away.
The river in itself is drowned,
And isles the astonished cattle round.

60
Let others tell the paradox,
How eels now bellow in the ox;
How horses at their tails do kick,
Turned as they hang to leeches quick;
How boats can over bridges sail;
And fishes do the stables scale.
How salmons trespassing are found;
480 And pikes are taken in the pound.

61
But I, retiring from the flood,
Take sanctuary in the wood;
And, while it lasts, myself embark

In this yet green, yet growing ark;
Where the first carpenter might best
Fit timber for his keel have pressed.
And where all creatures might have shares,
Although in armies, not in pairs.

62

The double wood of ancient stocks
Linked in so thick, an union locks,
It like two pedigrees appears,
On one hand Fairfax, the other Vere's:
Of whom though many fell in war,
Yet more to heaven shooting are:
And, as they nature's cradle decked,
Will in green age her hearse expect.

63

When first the eye this forest sees
It seems indeed as wood not trees:
As if their neighbourhood so old
To one great trunk them all did mould.
There the huge bulk takes place, as meant
To thrust up a fifth element;
And stretches still so closely wedged
As if the night within were hedged.

64

Dark all without it knits; within
It opens passable and thin;
And in as loose an order grows,
As the Corinthian porticos.
The arching boughs unite between
The columns of the temple green;
And underneath the winged choirs
Echo about their tuned fires.

65

The nightingale does here make choice
To sing the trials of her voice.
Low shrubs she sits in, and adorns
With music high the squatted thorns.
But highest oaks stoop down to hear,
And listening elders prick the ear.
The thorn, lest it should hurt her, draws
520   Within the skin its shrunken claws.

66

But I have for my music found
A sadder, yet more pleasing sound:
The stock-doves, whose fair necks are graced
With nuptial rings their ensigns chaste;
Yet always, for some cause unknown,
Sad pair unto the elms they moan.
O why should such a couple mourn,
That in so equal flames do burn!

67

Then as I careless on the bed
530   Of gelid strawberries do tread,
And through the hazels thick espy
The hatching throstle's shining eye,
The heron from the ash's top,
The eldest of its young lets drop,
As if it stork-like did pretend
That tribute to its Lord to send.

68

But most the hewel's wonders are,
Who here has the holt-felster's care.
He walks still upright from the root,
540   Measuring the timber with his foot;
And all the way, to keep it clean,
Doth from the bark the wood-moths glean.

He, with his beak, examines well
Which fit to stand and which to fell.

69

The good he numbers up, and hacks;
As if he marked them with the axe.
But where he, tinkling with his beak,
Does find the hollow oak to speak,
That for his building he designs,
550 And through the tainted side he mines.
Who could have thought the tallest oak
Should fall by such a feeble stroke!

70

Nor would it, had the tree not fed
A traitor-worm, within it bred.
(As first our flesh corrupt within
Tempts impotent and bashful sin.)
And yet that worm triumphs not long,
But serves to feed the hewel's young.
While the oak seems to fall content,
560 Viewing the treason's punishment.

71

Thus I, easy philosopher,
Among the birds and trees confer:
And little now to make me, wants
Or of the fowls, or of the plants.
Give me but wings as they, and I
Straight floating on the air shall fly:
Or turn me but, and you shall see
I was but an inverted tree.

72

Already I begin to call
570 In their most learned original:
And where I language want, my signs

The bird upon the bough divines;
And more attentive there doth sit
Than if she were with lime-twigs knit.
No leaf does tremble in the wind
Which I returning cannot find.

73
Out of these scattered sibyl's leaves
Strange prophecies my fancy weaves:
And in one history consumes,
580   Like Mexique paintings, all the plumes.
What Rome, Greece, Palestine, ere said
I in this light mosaic read.
Thrice happy he who, not mistook,
Hath read in nature's mystic book.

74
And see how chance's better wit
Could with a mask my studies hit!
The oak-leaves me embroider all,
Between which caterpillars crawl:
And ivy, with familiar trails,
590   Me licks, and clasps, and curls, and hales.
Under this antic cope I move
Like some great prelate of the grove,

75
Then, languishing with ease, I toss
On pallets swollen of velvet moss;
While the wind, cooling through the boughs,
Flatters with air my panting brows.
Thanks for my rest ye mossy banks,
And unto you cool zephyrs thanks,
Who, as my hair, my thoughts too shed,
600   And winnow from the chaff my head.

76

How safe, methinks, and strong, behind
These trees have I encamped my mind;
Where beauty, aiming at the heart,
Bends in some tree its useless dart;
And where the world no certain shot
Can make, or me it toucheth not.
But I on it securely play,
And gall its horsemen all the day.

77

Bind me ye woodbines in your twines,
610 Curl me about ye gadding vines,
And oh so close your circles lace,
That I may never leave this place:
But, lest your fetters prove too weak,
Ere I your silken bondage break,
Do you, O brambles, chain me too,
And courteous briars nail me through.

78

Here in the morning tie my chain,
Where the two woods have made a lane;
While, like a guard on either side,
620 The trees before their Lord divide;
This, like a long and equal thread,
Betwixt two labyrinths does lead.
But, where the floods did lately drown,
There at the evening stake me down.

79

For now the waves are fallen and dried,
And now the meadows fresher dyed;
Whose grass, with moister colour dashed,
Seems as green silks but newly washed.
No serpent new nor crocodile
630 Remains behind our little Nile;

Unless itself you will mistake,
Among these meads the only snake.

80

See in what wanton harmless folds
It everywhere the meadow holds;
And its yet muddy back doth lick,
Till as a crystal mirror slick;
Where all things gaze themselves, and doubt
If they be in it or without.
And for his shade which therein shines,
640   Narcissus-like, the sun too pines.

81

Oh what a pleasure 'tis to hedge
My temples here with heavy sedge;
Abandoning my lazy side,
Stretched as a bank unto the tide;
Or to suspend my sliding foot
On the osier's undermined root,
And in its branches tough to hang,
While at my lines the fishes twang!

82

But now away my hooks, my quills,
650   And angles, idle utensils.
The young Maria walks tonight:
Hide trifling youth thy pleasures slight.
'Twere shame that such judicious eyes
Should with such toys a man surprise;
She that already is the law
Of all her sex, her age's awe.

83

See how loose nature, in respect
To her, itself doth recollect;
And everything so whisht and fine,

660 Starts forthwith to its *bonne mine*.
The sun himself, of her aware,
Seems to descend with greater care;
And lest she see him go to bed;
In blushing clouds conceals his head.

84

So when the shadows laid asleep
From underneath these banks do creep,
And on the river as it flows
With ebon shuts begin to close;
The modest halcyon comes in sight,
670 Flying betwixt the day and night;
And such an horror calm and dumb,
Admiring nature does benumb.

85

The viscous air, wheresoe'er she fly,
Follows and sucks her azure dye;
The jellying stream compacts below,
If it might fix her shadow so;
The stupid fishes hang, as plain
As flies in crystal overta'en;
And men the silent scene assist,
680 Charmed with the sapphire-winged mist.

86

Maria such, and so doth hush
The world, and through the evening rush.
No new-born comet such a train
Draws through the sky, nor star new-slain.
For straight those giddy rockets fail,
Which from the putrid earth exhale,
But by her flames, in heaven tried,
Nature is wholly vitrified.

87

'Tis she that to these gardens gave
690   That wondrous beauty which they have;
She straightness on the woods bestows;
To her the meadow sweetness owes;
Nothing could make the river be
So crystal-pure but only she;
She yet more pure, sweet, straight, and fair,
Than gardens, woods, meads, rivers are.

88

Therefore what first she on them spent,
They gratefully again present.
The meadow carpets where to tread;
700   The garden flowers to crown her head;
And for a glass the limpid brook,
Where she may all her beauties look;
But, since she would not have them seen,
The wood about her draws a screen.

89

For she, to higher beauties raised,
Disdains to be for lesser praised.
She counts her beauty to converse
In all the languages as hers;
Nor yet in those herself employs
710   But for the wisdom, not the noise;
Nor yet that wisdom would affect,
But as 'tis heaven's dialect.

90

Blest Nymph! that couldst so soon prevent
Those trains by youth against thee meant;
Tears (watery shot that pierce the mind;)
And sighs (Love's cannon charged with wind;)
True praise (that breaks through all defence;)
And feigned complying innocence;

But knowing where this ambush lay,
720   She scaped the safe, but roughest way.

91

This 'tis to have been from the first
In a domestic heaven nursed,
Under the discipline severe
Of Fairfax, and the starry Vere;
Where not one object can come nigh
But pure, and spotless as the eye;
And goodness doth itself entail
On females, if there want a male.

92

Go now fond sex that on your face
730   Do all your useless study place,
Nor once at vice your brows dare knit
Lest the smooth forehead wrinkled sit:
Yet your own face shall at you grin,
Thorough the black-bag of your skin;
When knowledge only could have filled
And virtue all those furrows tilled.

93

Hence she with graces more divine
Supplies beyond her sex the line;
And, like a sprig of mistletoe,
740   On the Fairfacian oak does grow;
Whence, for some universal good,
The priest shall cut the sacred bud;
While her glad parents most rejoice,
And make their destiny their choice.

94

Meantime ye fields, springs, bushes, flowers,
Where yet she leads her studious hours,
(Till fate her worthily translates,

And find a Fairfax for our Thwaites)
Employ the means you have by her,
750 And in your kind yourselves prefer;
That, as all virgins she precedes,
So you all woods, streams, gardens, meads.

95
For you Thessalian Tempe's seat
Shall now be scorned as obsolete;
Aranjuez, as less, disdained;
The Bel-Retiro as constrained;
But name not the Idalian grove,
For 'twas the seat of wanton love;
Much less the dead's Elysian Fields,
760 Yet nor to them your beauty yields.

96
'Tis not, what once it was, the world;
But a rude heap together hurled;
All negligently overthrown,
Gulfs, deserts, precipices, stone.
Your lesser world contains the same.
But in more decent order tame;
You heaven's centre, nature's lap.
And paradise's only map.

97
But now the salmon-fishers moist
770 Their leathern boats begin to hoist;
And, like Antipodes in shoes,
Have shod their heads in their canoes.
How tortoise-like, but not so slow,
These rational amphibii go!
Let's in: for the dark hemisphere
Does now like one of them appear.

A DIALOGUE BETWEEN THYRSIS AND DORINDA

Dorinda	When death shall snatch us from these kids,
	And shut up our divided lids,
	Tell me Thyrsis, prithee do,
	Whither thou and I must go.
Thyrsis	To the Elysium: *Dorinda* oh where is't?
Thyrsis	A chaste soul, can never miss't.
Dorinda	I know no way, but one, our home;
	Is our cell Elysium?
Thyrsis	Cast thine eye to yonder sky.
10	There the milky way doth lie;
	'Tis a sure but rugged way,
	That leads to everlasting day.
Dorinda	There birds may nest, but how can I,
	That have no wings and cannot fly?
Thyrsis	Do not sigh (fair nymph) for fire
	Hath no wings, yet doth aspire
	Till it hit, against the pole,
	Heaven's the centre of the soul.
Dorinda	But in Elysium how do they
20	Pass eternity away?
Thyrsis	Oh, there's, neither hope nor fear
	There's no wolf, no fox, no bear.
	No need of dog to fetch our stray,
	Our Lightfoot we may give away;
	No oat-pipe's needful, there thine ears
	May feast with music of the spheres.
Dorinda	Oh sweet! oh sweet! How I my future state
	By silent thinking, antedate:
	I prithee let us spend, our time to come
30	In talking of Elysium.
Thyrsis	Then I'll go on: There, sheep are full
	Of softest grass, and softest wool;
	There, birds sing consorts, garlands grow,
	Cool winds do whisper, springs do flow.
	There, always is, a rising sun,

	And day is ever, but begun.
	Shepherds there, bear equal sway,
	And every nymph's a Queen of May.
Dorinda	Ah me, ah me. *Thyrsis* Dorinda, why dost cry?
Dorinda	I'm sick, I'm sick, and fain would die:
41	Convince me now, that this is true;
	By bidding, with me, all adieu.
Thyrsis	I cannot live, without thee, I
	Will for thee, much more with thee die.
Chorus	Then let us give Carillo charge o' the sheep,
	And thou and I'll pick poppies and them steep
	In wine, and drink on't even till we weep,
	So shall we smoothly pass away in sleep.

AN HORATIAN ODE UPON
CROMWELL'S RETURN FROM IRELAND

The forward youth that would appear
Must now forsake his muses dear,
    Nor in the shadows sing
    His numbers languishing.
'Tis time to leave the books in dust,
And oil the unused armour's rust:
    Removing from the wall
    The corslet of the hall.
So restless Cromwell could not cease
10   In the inglorious arts of peace,
    But through adventurous war
    Urged his active star.
And, like the three-forked lightning, first
Breaking the clouds where it was nursed,
    Did thorough his own side
    His fiery way divide.
For 'tis all one to courage high
    The emulous or enemy;

And with such to inclose
20   Is more than to oppose.
Then burning through the air he went,
And palaces and temples rent:
      And Caesar's head at last
      Did through his laurels blast.
'Tis madness to resist or blame
The force of angry heaven's flame:
      And, if we would speak true,
      Much to the man is due.
Who, from his private gardens, where
30   He lived reserved and austere,
      As if his highest plot
      To plant the bergamot,
Could by industrious valour climb
To ruin the great work of time,
      And cast the kingdom old
      Into another mould.
Though justice against fate complain,
And plead the ancient rights in vain:
      But those do hold or break
40   As men are strong or weak.
Nature that hateth emptiness,
Allows of penetration less:
      And therefore must make room
      Where greater spirits come.
What field of all the Civil Wars,
Where his were not the deepest scars?
      And Hampton shows what part
      He had of wiser art.
Where, twining subtle fears with hope,
50   He wove a net of such a scope,
      That Charles himself might chase
      To Carisbrooke's narrow case.
That thence the royal actor born
The tragic scaffold might adorn:
      While round the armed bands

Did clap their bloody hands.
He nothing common did or mean
Upon that memorable scene:
    But with his keener eye
60   The axe's edge did try:
Nor called the gods with vulgar spite
To vindicate his helpless right,
    But bowed his comely head,
    Down as upon a bed.
This was that memorable hour
Which first assured the forced power.
    So when they did design
    The Capitol's first line,
A bleeding head where they begun,
70   Did fright the architects to run;
    And yet in that the State
    Foresaw its happy fate.
And now the Irish are ashamed
To see themselves in one year tamed:
    So much one man can do,
    That does both act and know.
They can affirm his praises best,
And have, though overcome, confessed
    How good he is, how just,
80   And fit for highest trust:
Nor yet grown stiffer with command,
But still in the Republic's hand:
    How fit he is to sway
    That can so well obey.
He to the Commons' feet presents
A kingdom, for his first year's rents:
    And, what he may, forbears
    His fame to make it theirs:
And has his sword and spoils ungirt,
90   To lay them at the public's skirt.
    So when the falcon high
    Falls heavy from the sky,

She, having killed, no more does search,
But on the next green bough to perch;
    Where, when he first does lure,
    The falconer has her sure.
What may not then our isle presume
While Victory his crest does plume!
    What may not others fear
100   If thus he crown each year!
A Caesar he ere long to Gaul,
To Italy an Hannibal,
    And to all states not free
    Shall climacteric be.
The Pict no shelter now shall find
Within his parti-coloured mind;
    But from this valour sad
    Shrink underneath the plaid:
Happy if in the tufted brake
110 The English hunter him mistake;
    Nor lay his hounds in near
    The Caledonian deer.
But thou the war's and fortune's son
March indefatigably on;
    And for the last effect
    Still keep thy sword erect:
Besides the force it has to fright
The spirits of the shady night,
    The same arts that did gain
120 A power must it maintain.

FURTHER READING: A complete bibliography of studies of Marvell would fill very many pages. The following list is a selection of the most influential and/or instructive contributions.

Bradbrook, M. C., and Lloyd Thomas, M. G., *Andrew Marvell* (1940). A brief introductory critical account; now rather dated, but enjoyable to read.

Brooks, Cleanth, 'Literary Criticism', *English Institute Essays* (1946), pp. 127-58. On the 'ambiguity' of the 'Horatian Ode'; also 'A Note on the Limits of "History" and the Limits of "Criticism" ', *Sewanee Review*, 61 (1953), 129-35. Brooks's riposte to Bush's riposte.

Bush, Douglas, 'Marvell's "Horatian Ode" ', *Sewanee Review*, 60 (1952), 363-76. On the 'fallacy' of Brooks's argument.

Eliot, T. S., 'Andrew Marvell', *Times Literary Supplement*, 31 March 1921. Reprinted in *Selected Essays* of Eliot (1932). A very influential essay.

Empson, William, 'Marvell's Garden', *Some Versions of Pastoral* (1935). Finest example of intellectual brilliance or lunacy, depending on your point of view.

Friedman, Donald M., *Marvell's Pastoral Art* (1970). Perhaps the best of modern full-length studies.

Hauser, A., *Mannerism: The Crisis of the Renaissance and the Origin of Modern Art*, 2 vols. (1965). Primarily on the visual arts, but stimulating on Marvell, if not on all the literary texts he discusses.

Legouis, P., *Andrew Marvell: Poet, Puritan, Patriot* (1965). Abridged version of a work published in French in 1928; good biography and criticism from a conservative, no-nonsense point of view.

Leishman, J. B., *The Art of Marvell's Poetry* (1966). Erudite and graceful on the sources and traditions Marvell uses.

Martz, Louis L., *The Wit of Love* (1969). A short essay on Marvell develops Hauser's suggestions.

Toliver, H. E., *Marvell's Ironic Vision* (1965). Perhaps the best, if doomed, attempt to impose philosophic vision on Marvell's poetry.

Wilding, Michael, ed., *Marvell: Modern Judgements* (1969). Useful collection of essays, including three items listed above (Brooks's first essay, Bush's reply and Eliot's important essay), and an earlier version of Empson's account of 'The Garden'.